T0315658

NOTES ON IDENTIFICATION OF AEROPLANES.

(Issued by the General Staff.)

FireStep
Editions

www.firesteppublishing.com

August, 1917.

FireStep Publishing
Gemini House
136-140 Old Shoreham Road
Brighton
BN3 7BD

www.firesteppublishing.com

First published by the General Staff, War Office 1917.
First published in this format by FireStep Editions,
an imprint of FireStep Publishing, in association with
the National Army Museum, 2013.

NATIONAL
ARMY
MUSEUM

www.nam.ac.uk

ISBN 978-1-908487-86-5

Cover design FireStep Publishing
Typeset by FireStep Publishing
Printed and bound in Great Britain

Please note: *In producing in facsimile from original historical documents, any imperfections may be
reproduced and the quality may be lower than modern
typesetting or cartographic standards.*

NOTES ON IDENTIFICATION OF AEROPLANES.

DEFINITIONS.

Monoplane.—An aeroplane with one wing on each side of the body.

Biplane.—An aeroplane with two wings on each side of the body.

Triplane.—An aeroplane with three wings on each side of the body.

Tractor Machines.—Machines having the airscrew in front of the wings.

Pusher Machines.—Machines having the airscrew behind the wings.

Nacelle.—The term used in pusher machines for the body which carries the engine, controls, observer and pilot. The Caudron, although it is a tractor, is constructed after the pusher type. In " pusher " machines, the Nacelle projects well in front of the wings.

Under carriage.—The part of the structure connecting the wheels to the Nacelle.

Fuselage.—The body of a tractor machine, which carries the pilot, observer and engine, and extends back as far as the tail. All fuselages now, are covered with canvas or 3-ply wood.

Tail.—The small horizontal plane at the end of the fuselage.

Rudder.—The small vertical plane or planes attached to the tail.

Fin.—A small vertical fixed plane on the top of the fuselage and tail. The rudder is usually attached to the near end of the fin.

Dihedral.—An aeroplane is said to have Dihedral when the wings, as seen from the front, are set at angle to each other on either side of the body.

Stagger.—An aeroplane is said to have Stagger when the lower wings are not set vertically below the upper wings. ▪

Leading Edge.—The front edge of the wings of an aeroplane.

Trailing Edge.—The rear edge of the wings of an aeroplane.

Ailerons.—Flaps fitted to the trailing edge of the main plane in order to give lateral control. Ailerons are sometimes very conspicuous.

Overhang or Extensions.—An aeroplane is said to have Overhang when the upper wings are longer than the lower wings.

Sweep Back.—An aeroplane is said to be Swept Back when the wings, as seen from above or below, are not set in a straight line. Sometimes the leading edge is Swept Back whilst the trailing edge is straight.

Cut Back.—When the trailing edge is longer than the leading edge.

Wedge Shape.—When the leading edge is longer than the trailing edge.

Struts.—The wooden supports joining the upper wings to the lower wings.

These Notes should be studied in conjunction with the latest edition of " Silhouettes of Aeroplanes."

GENERAL INSTRUCTIONS.

1. Success in the identification of Aeroplanes can only be attained by an exact knowledge of the characteristics of the different types of 'plane, and by constant practice in observing all types of machines at all angles of flight.

Machines which can easily be identified at some angles often present at other angles no distinguishing characteristics to any but a trained observer. In order to pick up the characteristics of the different types the observer should employ a definite system of identification, and he should be acquainted with the specific purpose for which each type is employed.

Even a moderately trained observer should be able to distinguish between a hostile and a friendly machine at a distance of not less than 5,000 yards. If an observer is not able to do this, machine gun detachments will continually be having to " stand to " only to dismiss a minute later when it is realised that the 'plane is friendly: whilst for anti-aircraft artillery work it is essential that on a clear day 'planes should be identified at ranges of not less than 10,000 yards.

CLASSIFICATION.

2. Aeroplanes can be divided into two main classes: those designed for reconnaissance, artillery observation and bombing work, and those designed as chasers and scouts.

The former are usually comparatively large, stable, two-seater machines. Modern two-seater machines have a speed as high as 120 m.p.h. The R.E. 8 has a speed of about 90 m.p.h.

Although Artillery machines may fly at heights from 8,000 to 10,000 feet, the machines doing long reconnaissance will frequently get much higher, i.e., to 18,000 feet.

Scouts are smaller and faster machines, carrying a pilot only. Their flying speed is anything from 80 to 140 miles an hour ; the normal height for scouts is over 12,000 feet, and for the later types usually over 15,000 feet. These machines are essentially fighters, and by adopting offensive tactics on the enemy side of the lines seek to prevent his machines from doing their work and to enable our own to do theirs. Very often they fly at great heights in order to be able to dive effectively on to slower machines flying at lower heights.

CHARACTERISTICS.

3.   Many Allied machines employ tail booms, whilst up to date there are no German machines of this type of construction.   No doubt therefore should be entertained of any machine having an open structure connecting the wings to the tail.   This open structure is frequently referred to as "open fuselage.".

The Wings, being the most conspicuous part of an aeroplane, are usually examined first.

The special characteristics of British reconnaissance machines are Dihedral and Stagger; of French reconnaissance machines, Great Span, *i.e.*, length from wing tip to wing tip compared to width of planes, and open tail booms; of German reconnaissance machines, Overhang with Closed Fuselage.   In the majority of modern German machines the top and bottom planes are of equal length.

Only (four) Allied machines when flying shew both these German characteristics.   They are, B.E. 2.E., R.E. 8, Caudron R. 4, and Caudron G. 6.

With regard to the scouting class it is impossible to lay down any hard and fast rule by the wings alone.

The Tail and Rudder, for most types, are the surest guide for distinguishing Allied from hostile machines.

The vast majority of Allied machines have rectangular or modified rectangular tails, whilst the German machines have in most cases either the fish tail or the heart-shaped tail.

These distinctions apply equally to reconnaissance and scout machines.

4. MACHINES EMPLOYED FOR RECONNAISSANCE WORK.

ALLIED.

F.E. 2b.
F.E. 2d.
B.E. 2e.
R.E. 8.
MORANE PARASOL.
MARTINSYDE.
ARMSTRONG WHITWORTH BEARDMORE.
DE HAVILLAND 4.
BRISTOL FIGHTER.
HANDLEY PAGE.
VOISIN.
MAURICE FARMAN.
FARMAN FRERÈS.
SINGLE CAUDRON.
TWIN CAUDRON.
CAUDRON R. 4.
CAUDRON G. 6.
PAUL SCHMITT.
AVION A.R.
LETORD.
FRENCH MORANE.
MOINEAU.

GERMAN.

ALBATROS.
AVIATIK.
D.F.W. AVIATIK.
RUMPLER.
L.V.G.
GOTHA.
NEW TYPE.

MACHINES EMPLOYED FOR FIGHTING PURPOSES.

DE HAVILLAND 5.
SOPWITH BIPLANE.
SOPWITH SCOUT.
SOPWITH TRIPLANE.
SOPWITH CAMEL.
S.E. 5 with clipped wings.
*NIEUPORT.
*S.P.A.D.
†MORANE MONOCOQUE.

FOKKER.
ROLAND.
HALBERSTADTER.
ALBATROS SCOUT No. 1.
ALBATROS SCOUT No. 2.
S.S.W.

* Flown by both British and French.   † Flown by French only.

6

WINGS.

5. In examining the Wings of an Aeroplane there are six characteristics for which the observer should be on the look-out :—

(a) DIHEDRAL.
(b) SWEEP BACK.
(c) STAGGER.

(d) OVERHANG.
(e) WING TIPS.
(f) AILERONS.

6. Dihedral is most noticeable in a machine coming straight in or going away. It is also distinctly noticeable when travelling obliquely, but, at certain angles, machines with Swept Back wings may appear to have Dihedral. Care is required to differentiate between these two characteristics.

7. Sweep Back is seldom noticeable until a machine has reached an Angle of Sight of about 45°, except when banking. A very critical examination should always be made of a machine when banking, as many special characteristics such as the shape of the Wing Tips and Tail can then be best observed.

The Nieuport is, at present, the only Allied 'plane having Swept Back wings.

8. Stagger is most conspicuous when an Aeroplane is travelling obliquely or at right angles to the observer; in those positions the inclination of the struts is very obvious.

The effect of Stagger is to cause the planes to appear rather wide apart.

The Roland and Halberstadter machines have slight Stagger; otherwise Stagger can be regarded as a characteristic of Allied aeroplanes. In the De Havilland 5, Avion A.R. and Letord the Stagger is reversed, i.e., the top plane is behind the lower plane.

9. Overhang is best seen when a machine is coming straight in or going away. On oblique courses it is difficult to decide whether a machine has Overhang or not.

10. Wing Tips may be divided into four main classes : Round, Square, Cut Back, and Wedge Shape.

The Wings of British machines are chiefly of the Round, Cut Back, and Wedge Shape types, the only exception being the S.P.A.D.

French machines have either Square or Cut Back Tips.

Many German machines have Square Tips, but the Fokker, Roland, Halberstadter and Albatros Scout No. 2 have the Cut Back type.

11. Ailerons.—Few machines have Ailerons which can be detected from the ground, with the noticeable exception of the Voisin.

Old types of Albatros had noticeable Ailerons. These took the form of a thickening of the wing tips A look-out should be kept for Ailerons in new pattern German machines.

TAILS.

12. There are five main types of Tail, although there are many variations of these types.

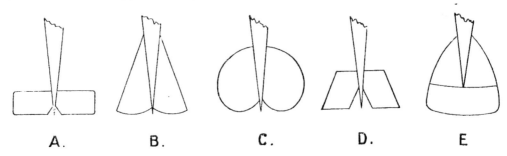

A.   B.   C.   D.   E

Type " A " is the rectangular. It is by far the commonest British type. It becomes modified into the following three types :—

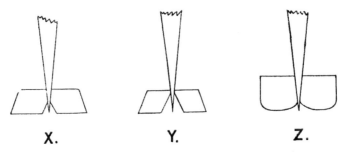

X.   Y.   Z.

Two German machines, the Halberstadter and the Fokker, have tails of type " Y."

Types " B " and " C " are essentially German, but one British machine, the De Havilland, has a tail of type " C "

Type " C " has developed into type " E ", which is now one of the commonest types of hostile tails.

Type " D " is employed by two Allied machines, the Nieuport and Moineau, and by one German machine, the Roland Scout.

Tails can best be observed when a machine is banking, or is directly overhead.

SHORT DESCRIPTION OF AEROPLANES.

BRITISH.

F.E. 2b. and 2d.—There are a considerable number of machines of this type. They are easily distinguished by their large size, Open Tail Booms, and marked Dihedral. The engine also has a loud purr, which is readily distinguishable after a time.

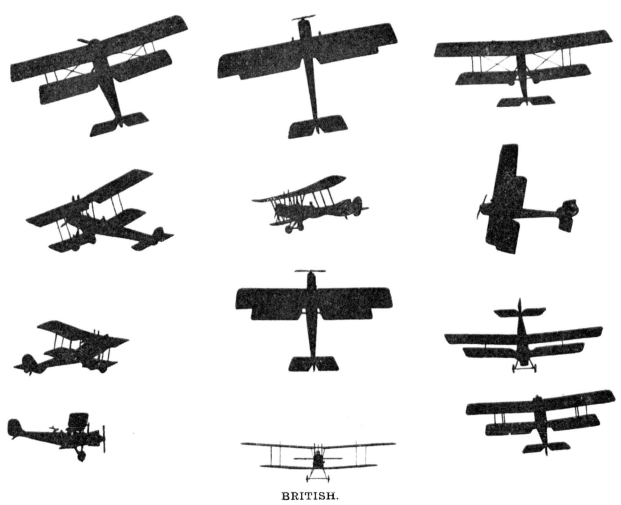

BRITISH.

B.E. 2.E. and R.E. 8.—These machines, except for a difference in the Rudders, are difficult to distinguish. Their characteristics are, marked Stagger, Dihedral, and Overhang, and the particularly blunt, Cut Back Tips to their wings. The engine is fairly silent.

The Rudder of the R.E. 8 joins the Fuselage almost at right angles, whilst that of the B.E. 2.E. has a Fin in front of it which slopes away to the Fuselage.

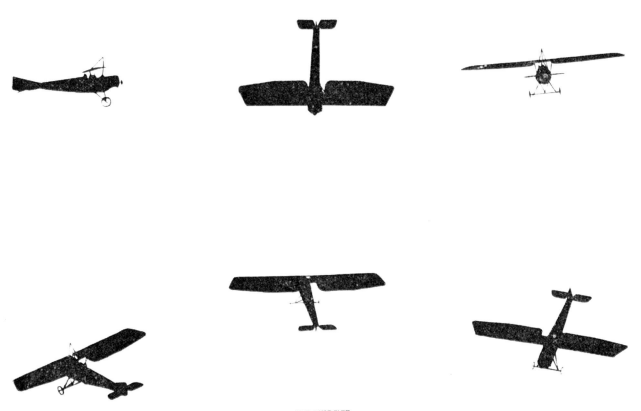

BRITISH.

Morane Parasol.—The Morane Parasol is a large two-seater monoplane with the Fuselage suspended well below the wings, giving it the form of a cross when approaching and receding.

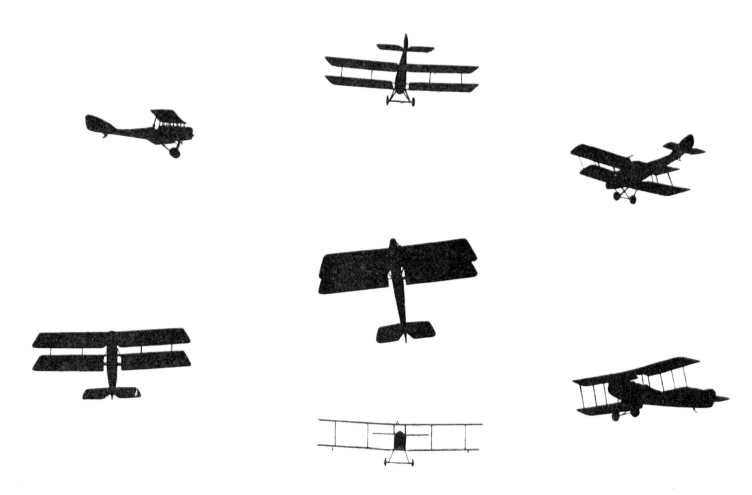

BRITISH.

Martinsyde.—The Martinsyde is a twin-seater used for bombing purposes. It has slight Dihedral and Stagger, deep wings with a marked cut-away by the Fuselage, and pronounced cut back wing tips. It has a tail of type " X " (para. 12).

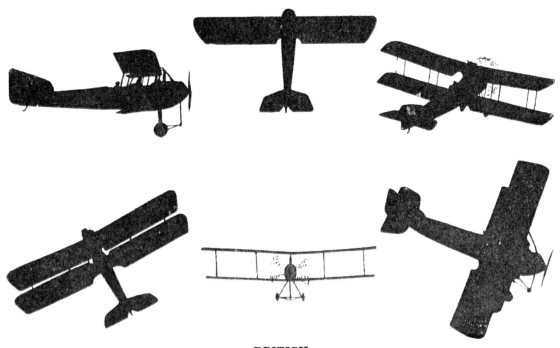

BRITISH.

Armstrong Whitworth.—This is very similar to a B.E. 2.c. but it is larger, and the planes have a much greater width from front to rear in proportion to their length (from wing tip to wing tip), the tips being markedly wedge shaped.

DE HAVILLAND. 4.

BRITISH.

De Havilland 4.—This machine is also similar to the B.E. 2c., but the nose is very square and projects a considerable distance in front of the planes.

The tail plane is also slightly different, and the wing tips are cut back.

BRISTOL FIGHTER

190 H.P.
TRACTOR BIPLANE

BRITISH.

Bristol Fighter.—The Bristol Fighter is a two-seater tractor biplane, with Closed Fuselage.

The leading edges of the planes are longer than the trailing edges, the tips of the wings are rounded, it has Dihedral and Stagger, and the tail is of type "D" (para. 12), but with the corners rounded off.

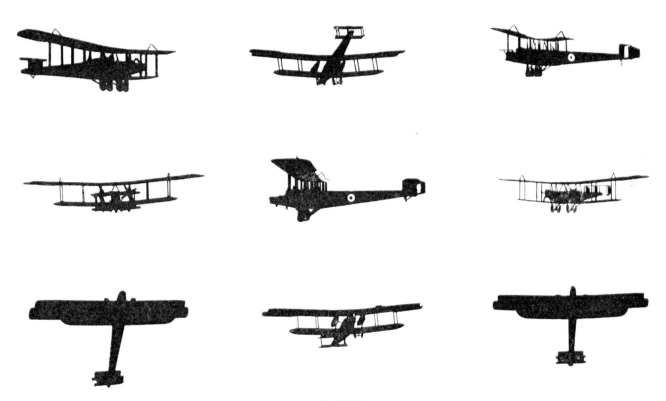

BRITISH.

Handley Page.—Single Fuselage Machine with Biplane Tail and Elevator.

Two Rudders, one on each side of the Fuselage mounted between top and bottom tail planes.

Two Engines mounted Stream line Nascelles, projecting beyond the Chord of the Planes on either side of the main body and driving Tractor Propellers.

At close ranges the projection formed by the "balance" portion of the Aileron is very marked.

From the ground tail appears to be very small and the front of the Fuselage snout-like in appearance.

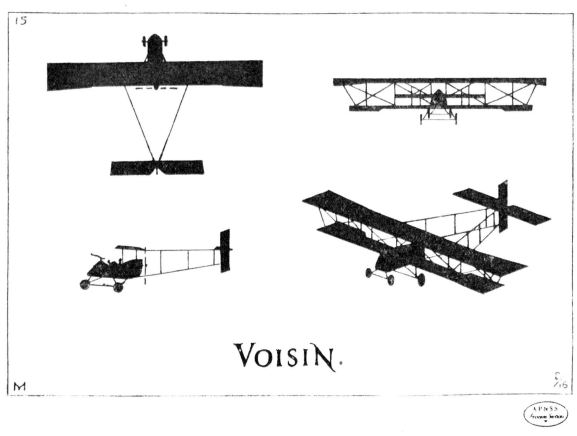

VOISIN.

FRENCH.

Voisin.—The Voisin is another large open tail booms machine, chiefly flown on long reconnaissance.s It is easily picked up by its marked Ailerons, and by its long and narrow tail. The tail, with the long narrow rudder, forms a perfect cross. It has Slight Overhang. This machine has a very noisy engine. The planes are very long in comparison with the vertical distance between them.

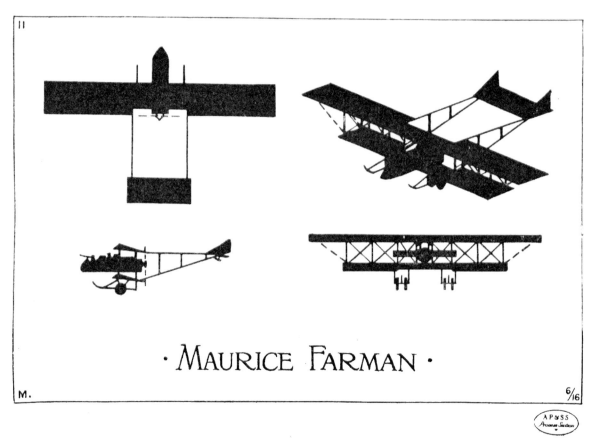

FRENCH.

The **Maurice Farman** is a large open tail booms reconnaissance machine. It is noticeable for its very square Wing Tips and large Overhang. Also for the fact that the struts of the Fuselage joined to the extremities of the large rectangular tail, are parallel. It has two rudders on top of the tail.

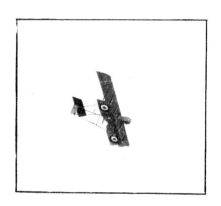

FRENCH.

Farman Freres.—The Farman Freres is a large open tail booms reconnaissance machine with a big Overhang. It can be readily identified by its Cut Back Wing Tips, Cut Back Tail, and the long rudder which is entirely below the tail.

FRENCH.

Single Caudron.—The single engine Caudron is not flown much nowadays. It is an open tail booms machine with a big Overhang. The tail is rectangular with a big piece cut out, having two rudders on top of it.

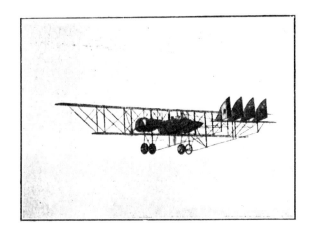

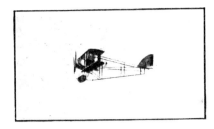

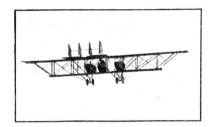

FRENCH.

Twin Caudron.—The double-engined Caudron is a reconnaissance machine, and is usually identified by its huge size, great Overhang, narrow wings, and twin engines. It is an open tail booms machine, and is remarkable for having four rudders on top of its large rectangular tail. (Type " A," para. 12.)

FRENCH.

Caudron R. 4.—The Caudron R. 4 is another twin engine reconnaissance machine of very large size. It has very long and narrow wings with a Slight Overhang, and has a Closed Fuselage. The tail is rectangular, very long and narrow, type "Y" (para. 12), with a single rudder and fin.

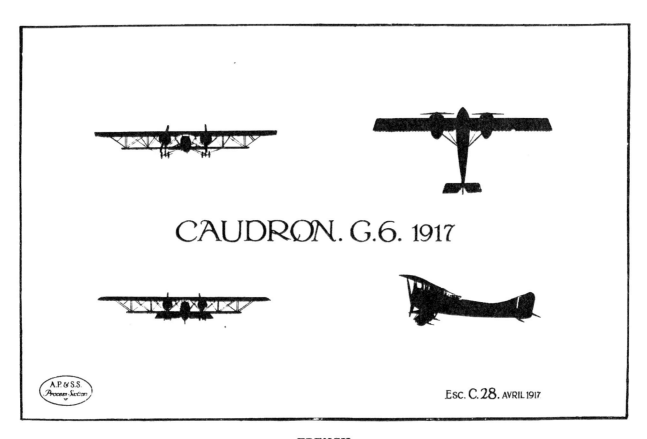

CAUDRON. G.6. 1917

ESC. C.28. AVRIL 1917

A.P. & S.S.
Process Section

FRENCH.

The Caudron G. 6 is a large twin-engine tractor reconnaissance machine, with a big Overhang, closed Fuselage and tail of Type " Y."

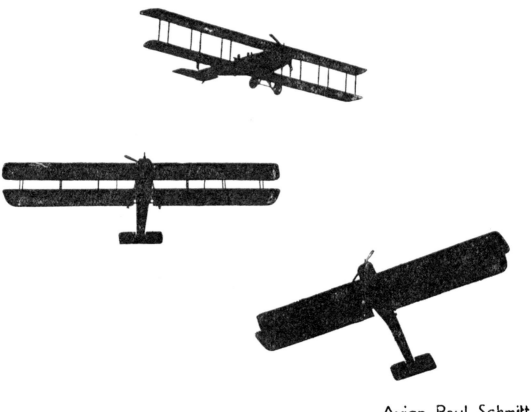

Avion Paul Schmitt
S. B. R., Type VI,

FRENCH.

The Paul Schmitt (Type VI.) is a big tractor reconnaissance machine, with closed fuselage, rectangular tail, and square rudder. The tips of the upper plane are cut back, and those of the lower plane wedge shaped.

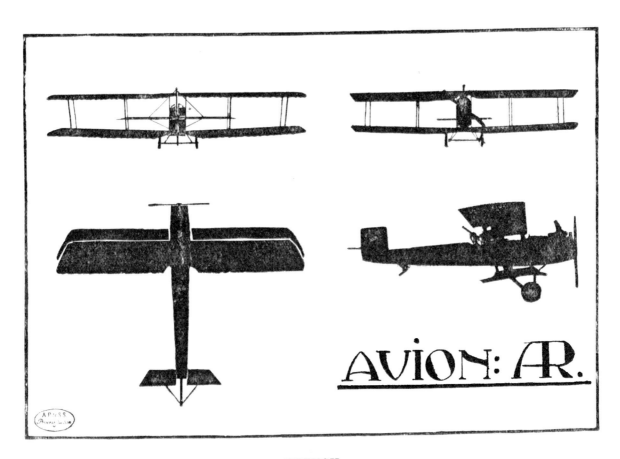

FRENCH.

    The Avion A.R. is a tractor biplane of ordinary size. It has reversed Stagger, slight Dihedral on the lower plane, closed Fuselage, large square rudder, and small tail similar to Type "Y."

FRENCH.

The Letord is a very large twin-engine, reconnaissance machine. It has Overhang and reversed Stagger, but no Dihedral. The wing tips are square cut. There is a noticeable cut-away on each side of the Fuselage, which is closed. The tail and rudder are particularly large.

FRENCH.

The French Morane is a very large, three-seater, twin-engine biplane. It has slight overhang, no dihedral, and no stagger. The wing tips are cut back and there are five pairs of struts (including the engines) on each side of the fuselage. The fuselage, tail, and rudder are of the ordinary Morane type.

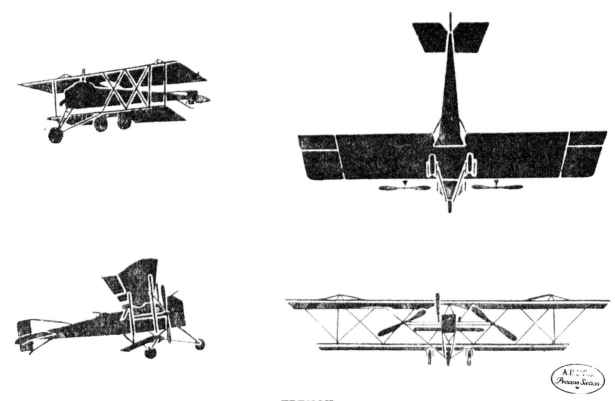

FRENCH.

The Moineau is a three-seater reconnaissance machine. It has overhang, but neither stagger nor dihedral. The wing tips are square cut; it has one pair of struts on each side of the fuselage, which is closed, and the bracing wires are very conspicuous. It has two tractor propellers geared to one engine. The tail is of type "D"; the fin is triangular, and the rudder is rectangular, very little of it projecting below the tail.

GERMAN.

Albatros.—The Albatros is the commonest of all German machines, and is a fast reconnaissance type. It can be picked up by its Overhang, squarish wing tips, and very large fish tail, type "B" (para. 12). It has a large fin and rudder above the tail, and flies, as many German machines do, with its tail well cocked up in the air.

The latest type Albatros have not got the overhang, and the tail is of a blunter, more rounded fish type.

GERMAN.

Aviatik.—The Aviatik is also very similar to the Albatros, the main difference being the tail, which is kidney-shaped. (Type "C," para. 12.) The wings are slightly Swept Back.

These three German reconnaissance machines are all very similar, and close observation is needed to differentiate one from the other. However, by reason of their Overhang, coupled with the Closed Fuselage, their large and easily distinguished tails, and their habits of flying with the latter cocked up, they are not difficult to recognise as hostile machines.

D.F.W. Aviatik.

Photo: Section
Nº I. A.D.

GERMAN.

The **D.F.W. Aviatik** is a machine with planes of equal length, no Stagger, and no Dihedral. The tips of the upper plane are cut back, and those of the lower plane wedge shaped. The tail is of a rounded, fish-like appearance—a cross between the Albatros and Aviatik types.

RUMPLER c

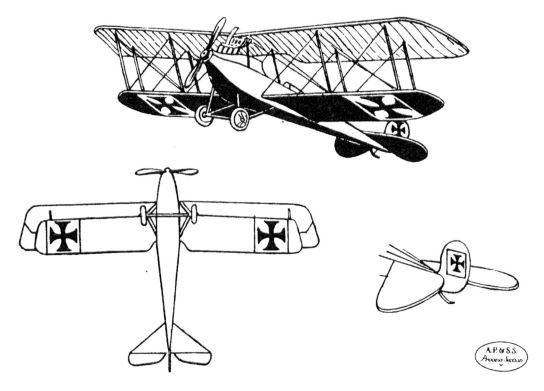

GERMAN.

The Rumpler is a two-seater tractor machine with slight Overhang; the upper plane is cut back, and the lower plane nearly square. The tail is of the fish type.

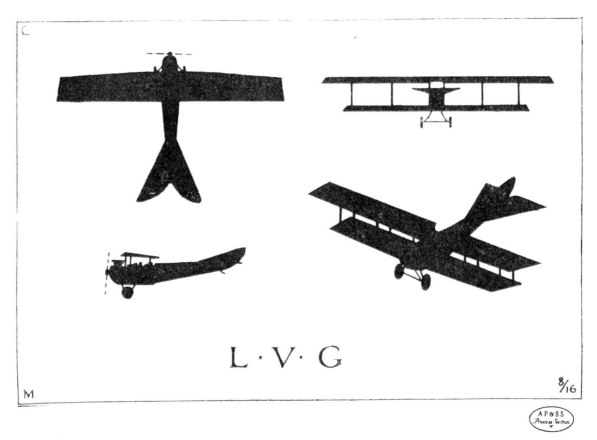

L · V · G

GERMAN.

L.V.G.—The L.V.G. is similar to the Albatros except that it is somewhat larger, with a more pronounced Overhang. The leading edges of the wings are markedly Swept Back.

Abt. Flugzeugwerke Gotha.

GERMAN.

The Gotha is a very large twin-engine machine. The wings are markedly swept back and have a slight Overhang. The Fuselage is closed and the tail and rudder are very distinctive, as under.

TAIL.   RUDDER AND FIN.

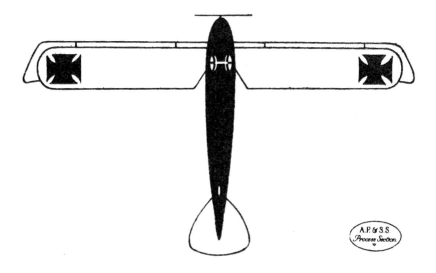

GERMAN.

New Type (probably Albatros).—This machine has slight Overhang and no Dihedral or Stagger. The upper plane is cut back, the lower plane rounded. The tail is of the Albatros Scout, type and the rudder of the ordinary Albatros type.

DE HAVILLAND 5
TRACTOR BIPLANE
REVERSED STAGGER

BRITISH.

De Havilland 5.—The De Havilland 5 is a unique British type in that it has a reversed Stagger. It also has a closed Fuselage.

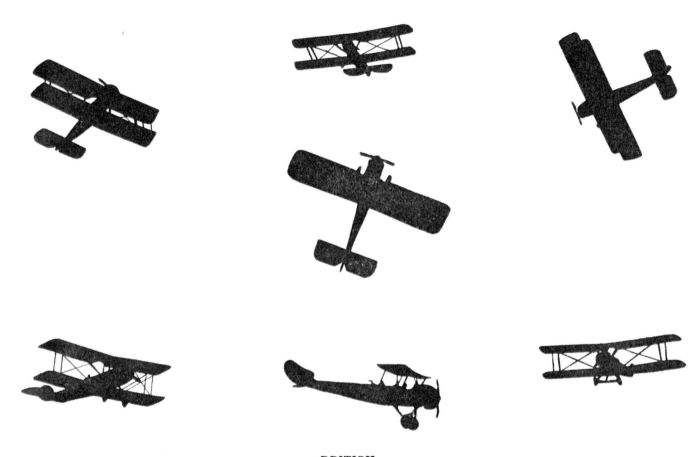

BRITISH.

Sopwith Biplane.—The Sopwith Biplane is a small and fast two-seater machine. It may be distinguished by Closed Fuselage, Slight Dihedral, Stagger, and kidney-shaped Rudder. It is also the only machine with a tail of type "Z" (para. 12). The engine has a loud and distinctive ringing note.

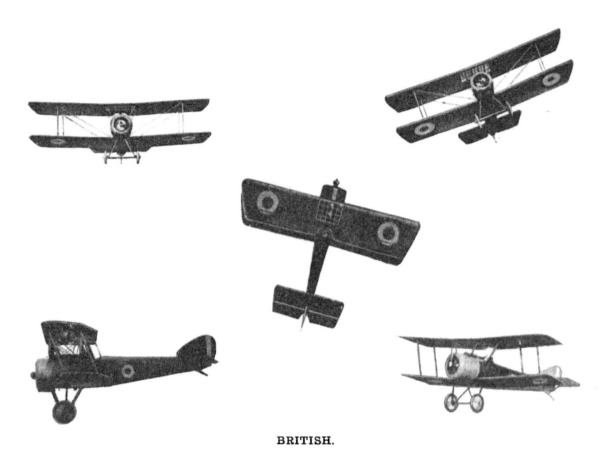

BRITISH.

Sopwith Scout.—The Sopwith Scout is a fast one-seater machine. The Wing Tips and Tail are wedge shaped. It has Stagger, Dihedral, and Closed Fuselage.

BRITISH.

Sopwith Triplane.—The Sopwith Triplane has three planes, and the wing tips are cut as in the Scout except that the corners are very slightly rounded. The tail and rudder are similar to those of the Sopwith Scout.

BRITISH.

The Sopwith Camel is a small, single-seater machine. It has Stagger, but no Overhang. The upper plane is straight, but the lower has a marked Dihedral, the tips of both being cut back. The tail is of Type "X," and the rudder is similar to that of the Sopwith Scout.

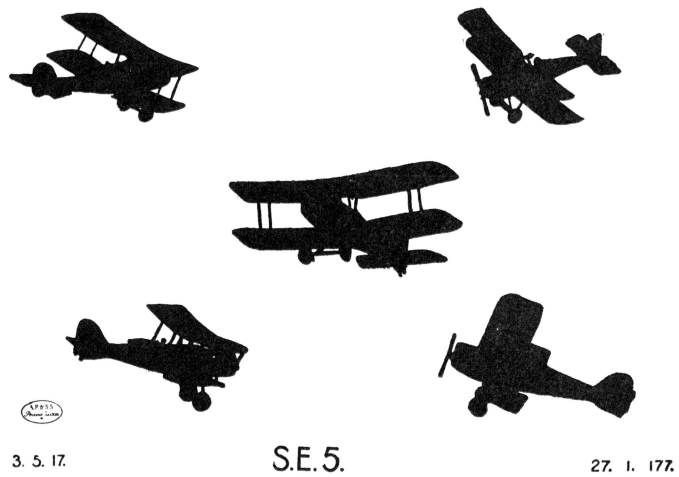

3. 5. 17.

S.E.5.

BRITISH.

27. 1. 177.

  The S.E. 5 is a single-seater tractor biplane. It has a marked Dihedral and Stagger ; the tips of the wings almost square cut, no overhang and one pair of struts on either side.
  The tail is the same as the R.E. 8, but the rudder is large and triangular with the top point cut off. Care must be taken not to mistake the machine for the Halberstadter.

BRITISH.

Nieuport.—The Nieuport is a fast, single-seater Scout, very difficult to identify at certain angles.

Its most marked peculiarity is the very narrow under-plane, which is shorter than the upper-plane and has Dihedral. Once this is picked up doubt is at an end, but when coming straight in, the Overhang and Dihedral of the under-plane give it an extremely Hun-like appearance.

The tail is of type " D " (para. 12) and must be carefully watched, but the rudder, which is on top of the tail and projects well in rear of it, is easily distinguishable. The wings are slightly Swept Back and the narrow under-plane necessitates a distinctive placing of the struts, thus—

Despite these numerous peculiarities the Nieuport has many times been mistaken for a German machine, and should always be carefully watched.

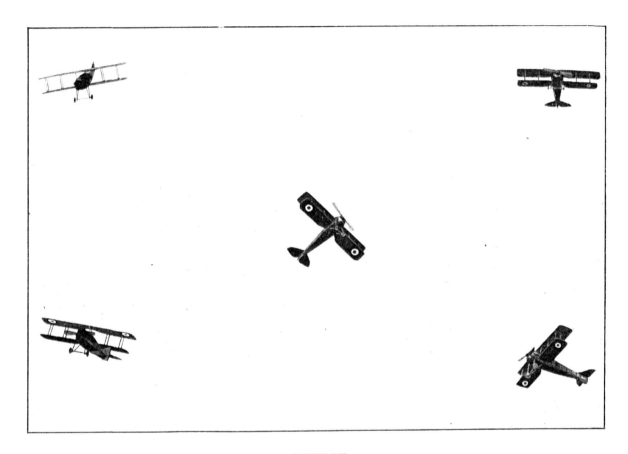

BRITISH.

S.P.A.D.—The S.P.A.D. is a tractor biplane, with Closed Fuselage, and is perhaps the most difficult of all Allied 'planes to distinguish.

The wings are square cut; there are two pairs of struts on either side of the nacelle which appear to be of equal length, but in reality there is a slight Overhang.

The tail (*see* sketch) is the safest guide to the identity of this machine.

The S.P.A.D. is liable to be mistaken for a hostile 'plane by unskilled observers, and the greatest care must therefore be exercised in establishing its identity.

MORANE MONOCOQUE
French single-seater tractor monoplane.

A.P.&S.S.
Process Section

C.G 13 April 1917

FRENCH.

The **Morane Monocoque** is a single-seater monoplane flown by the French. It is not a parasol. The wing tips are cut back, and there is no piece of the planes cut away near the fuselage. The tail is of Type " Y," the rudder projecting considerably beyond it.

GERMAN.

Fokker.—The Fokker is a fast monoplane Scout, having Cut Back Wings and rectangular Tail, type "Y" (para. 12). The round Rudder cocked up above the tail is its chief characteristic.

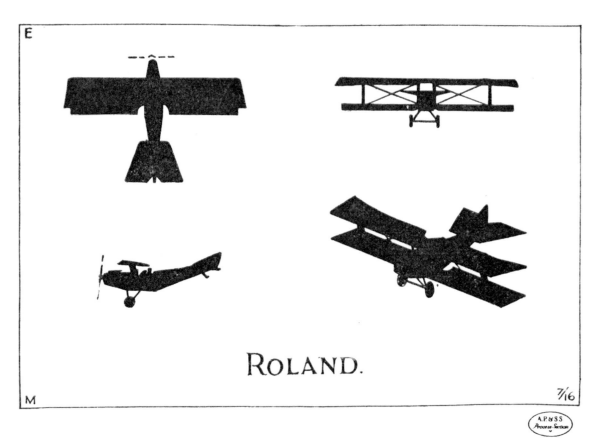

ROLAND.

7/16

GERMAN.

Roland.—The Roland scout is a fast machine. Its peculiarity is that it has one large strut on each side of the Fuselage in place of the usual pair. The rudder is triangular, and the rather large tail is similar to type "D" (para. 12) with the rear edges rounded. This 'plane does not fly much nowadays.

48

GERMAN.

Halberstadter.—The Halberstadter is a difficult machine to identify unless seen sideways, and then its high, triangular rudder is extremely prominent. Some uncertainty exists as to the exact structure, but most observers agree as to the Slight Dihedral and Stagger, whilst the tail is certainly of type "Y" (para. 12), this having been a common cause of confusion when the machine first appeared.

As soon, however, as the rudder can be seen, no further doubt is possible.

GERMAN.

Albatros Scout.—The Albatros Scout is a small and very fast machine. It has a slight Overhang, but is most easily distinguished by its "pear tail," similar to type "C" (para. 12), although with a blunt end, there being no notch cut out in the middle for the rudder. It is very easy to mistake the S.P.A.D. for this machine if the tail is not visible, the chief point of difference being that the S.P.A.D. has two pairs of struts on each side of the Fuselage, and the Albatros Scout only one.

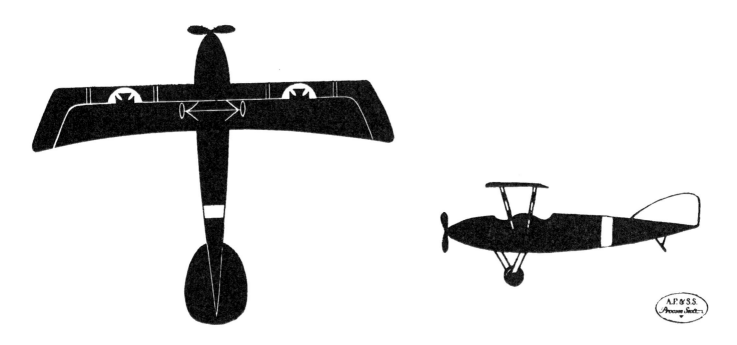

GERMAN.

The Albatros Scout No. 2. resembles in many points the Nieuport Scout. It has Overhang and a narrow under-plane, necessitating the same arrangement of struts as on the Nieuport. The planes are not swept back; the tips are markedly cut back. The rudder is a cross between the usual Albatros type and the Albatros Scout No. 1 type, while the tail is similar to that of the latter machine.

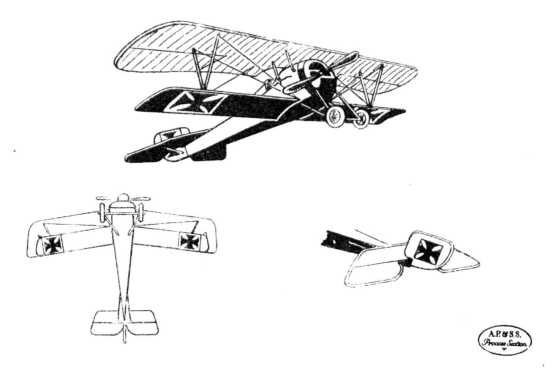

GERMAN.

The **S.S.W. (Siemens Schuckert Werke)** is almost an exact copy of the French Nieuport.

ND - #0534 - 270225 - C0 - 180/225/5 - PB - 9781908487865 - Matt Lamination